Introduction

The Jersey Shore is over 100 miles and extends into five counties. The fire apparatus that has served two of those counties is featured in this book. Monmouth and Ocean Counties are rich in history, and have had some of the most interesting fire apparatus to have served in this country.

Monmouth County, located at the northern area of the shore region, is the sixth largest county in New Jersey with 471 square miles and over 570,000 people. To the north it's bordered by the Raritan Bay (Lower New York Harbor), from Sandy Hook, the county's coast line runs to the Manasquan River. The County of Middlesex is to the northwest, Mercer and Burlington Counties are to the west, and Ocean County to the south. The Borough of Freehold, settled in 1713, is the county seat as well as the hometown of the rock singer Bruce Springsteen. The county was the site of General Washington's famed Battle of Monmouth, which commenced on June, 1778. Today, Monmouth County is a much quieter place, comprised of quaint shore towns, vast farmlands, forests, suburban sprawl, as well as a few small urban areas like the cities of Asbury Park and Long Branch. Monmouth County has 53 incorporated municipalities, with nearly 4000 volunteers and over 200 career fighters who operate from 125 stations.

Ocean County traces its roots back to 1850. These low lying coastal plains rank eleventh in population, while the county's land mass comes in number two at 638 square miles. Lakehurst, in the central part of the county, was the infamous location of the Hindenburg disaster. The German dirigible exploded, without warning on May 6, 1937, killing 36 persons. The County Seat, Toms River, was surveyed in 1673 and named after its founder Capt. William Tom. Today Ocean County has large areas of the New Jersey Pine Barrens, a protected forest area, as well as farmlands, seaside towns, summer resort areas, and suburban sprawl. The Atlantic Ocean is to the east, Atlantic and Burlington Counties, to the south and west. North of the Manasquan River is Monmouth County. The Fire Service in Ocean County is provided by over 1500 volunteers, and almost 80 career firefighters who serve 33 municipalities from 62 stations.

Dedication

This book is proudly dedicated to two of the finest fire apparatus photographers to have ever graced the hobby, William N. Schwartz and the late James P. Burner. These two men, who have a combined career in photography of well over one hundred years, could always be seen at parades and events throughout the Garden State. Bill has been a member of the E.H. Stokes Fire Company since 1937. He has served in all line officer and administrative positions, and also served two terms as the Chief of the Ocean Grover Fire Department. Jim Burner was a life member of the Oakhurst Independent Hose Company in Ocean Township before moving to Neptune City. Almost all of the black and white photography in this book is the product of these two men. Without them this project would not have been possible. These men are true pioneers in a hobby that has evolved from such humble beginnings. Bill, Jim, thanks for everything.

William N. Schwartz & James P. Burner
Princeton Junction, NJ
June 1998

Acknowledgments

The authors would gratefully like to thank the following:

Mr. Scott Mattson, an advocate of this book from it's very beginning, helped this project succeed in many ways. For example his excellent color slide photography, combined with his apparatus knowledge and his technical prowess, truly improved both the accuracy and the overall quality of this book.

Special Thanks to Jon Bentivegna, the founder of the Jersey Shore Fire Photographers Association, who helped unite the authors with his original apparatus newsletter the "Jersey Shore Firefleet". Without Jon, this book would not exist.

We would like to especially thank Jack Calderone, Jack DeRossett, John Toomey and John Systma. They granted us permission to use their wonderful photographs from theirspectacular collections.

We would like to give a special thank you to Michael Woortman, Dave Connelly and the staff of Contemporary Color. Contemporary Color's total support of this project along with their design, production, digital prepress, and printing have made this book a treasured collection.

John Rowe would like to personally thank his parents Carmeen and Jack, his sisters Jacquie and Nanci, their families, Lee Eggert, Cris Clark, Bob Hotmar, Bob Lewis, and Lynn Gebhardt for their support and encouragement.

John Reith would like to thank his parents Hank and Marion and grandmother, for all their support throughout the years. His fiancé Michele Lastoczy, for your patience and support, I love you. He would also like to thank John Maleky, Ron Jeffers, Div. Warden Maris Gabliks, Sect. Wardens Chris Irick, Dist. Warden Ray Mount.

Tim Regan would like to thank his wife Patti, who after helping him with five books, deserves a medal. My parents Betty and Gene, and my brother Dan, John Brandauer Ex - Chief Keyport F.D., Dave Galloway, Randy Stout, Jim McTernan and Emile Schettino.

And to all the firefighters who took the time to pose their rigs for the photographs and research the historical information.

PREFACE

The very first motorized fire apparatus to make its appearance on the New Jersey Shore, would arrive in the firehouse of the Liberty Hose Company of Red Bank in 1908. It was from the delivery of this very first vehicle that the age of motorized apparatus would sweep across the towns and villages of New Jersey, quickly replacing the hand and horse drawn vehicles of the 19th century.

In the beginning, firemen were hesitant to try out the motorized vehicles, just as they had been about replacing manpower with horses seventy five years earlier. However, it was every fire company's dream to be able to have an auto-truck, something they could be proud of, and it beat hauling the old gal around by hand at two o'clock in the morning to a fire three miles away. Red Bank's little Pope-Toledo laid the ground work and soon towns from Point Pleasant and Barnegat to Atlantic Highlands and Keyport were racing to motorize their fleets.

By the mid 1920's most fire departments had completely motorized their units. Most early fire apparatus were built using a luxury automobile chassis. They were more affordable than truck chassis, easily obtainable, not to mention reliable. Vehicles such as Locomobile, Cadillac and even foreign cars, such as Fiats were often sent off to the local body builder to be turned into a useful, yet spartan firefighting machine. Fire Companies who could not afford to purchase fire apparatus would sometimes mortgage their own houses in an effort to find the down payment for the purchase of these trucks. Fund raisers and fairs dominated the summer scene for the volunteers as ever increasing money would be needed to build and equip the motorized fire apparatus.

Most early apparatus had no fire pumps on them at all. They were usually built with chemical equipment which had been transferred from hand or horse drawn vehicles. A good example was Ocean Groves' 1909 Auto Car rig, whose equipment came from an 1890's Holloway Chemical wagon. Although chemical equipment was effective, it was slightly expensive. Commonly, early rigs were nothing more than hose wagons that carried nozzles and hose, relying on hydrant connections for firefighting.

A look in any firehouse during the first twenty five years of motorization would have boggled the minds of any enthusiast. With the myriad of names and styles of makes, combined with the frequency that these machines changed owners, made for some confusing times. Fire Departments began the tradition of selling their older rigs to newly formed neighboring fire companies. It was not uncommon for some trucks to have three or four careers before being retired.

In this volume everything from standard pumpers to aerial ladders to tractor drawn tankers and former military trucks can be seen. One-of-a-kind rigs, like Long Branch's Day-Elder and Union Beach's Stoughton are included, as well as Middletown Fire Company's Mack B triplets, a tanker, pumper and a quad.

Unique color schemes, such as the dark green of Breton Woods Fire Co. or the cream fleet of Wanamassa Fire Co., all combine to reflect the diversity of this regions former fire department fleets. This is truly an outstanding collection of fire apparatus photography from an area which is rich in fire service history, and known for utilizing some of the most progressive apparatus of the time. Rigs like Red Bank's 1965 Seagrave, were delivered with a 1500-gallon per minute pump, quite a feature for that time. Local built rigs are also included, such as Tasc, which was manufactured by Trautwein of Woodbridge. Tasc's may be found throughout New Jersey, mounted primarily on commercial truck chassis.

Fire Apparatus of the Jersey Shore is a cross section of fire apparatus of the area and has developed from the beginning of the century to the mid-1960's. It's a one of a kind ride, so pull up your bunkers, put your helmet on, and step on that siren. It's time to roll out and see some outstanding photography of some truly remarkable fire apparatus!

CONTENTS

Chapter I
1908 - 1929
Goodbye to the Horses

Chapter II
1930 - 1950
The Classic Fire Engine

Chapter III
1951 - 1965
Cab Overs, Diesels and the Modern Era

Chapter IV
The Survivors
Those Who Escaped the Scrapyard

Chapter I
1908 - 1929
Goodbye to the Horses

Engine Company No. 2 in Manasquan once ran this 1922 American LaFrance. Ole' Peg was finally retired in 1954 after thirty two years of continuous service. This unit has been restored and is still owned by Engine Co. No. 2.

Not much bigger than a bread box, this was the 1908 Pope-Toledo Hose Wagon. Proudly delivered to the Liberty Hose Co. No. 2 of the Red Bank Fire Department on October 12, 1908, this little rig was the first motorized unit in the shore area. Interestingly, this little rig could only hold four firemen plus the driver. To solve this problem four numbered paddles hung on the fire house wall and this determined who rode on the rig. Everyone else would have to start running.

In 1909 Ocean Grove placed this 48.5 horsepower Autocar chassis in service. Constructed in Buffalo, NY the unit's chemical equipment had been transferred from the company's 1891 Holloway chemical engine.

After removing the horse stalls from the building to make room for this "big" machine, the new motorized rig was backed into the station, much to the delight of the boy's at the E.H. Stokes Fire Company. This fancy rig must have commanded quite a presence while racing to calls in the first part of the 20th century.

Jersey Shore Fire Apparatus Volume 1 "Classics thru the 60's"   07

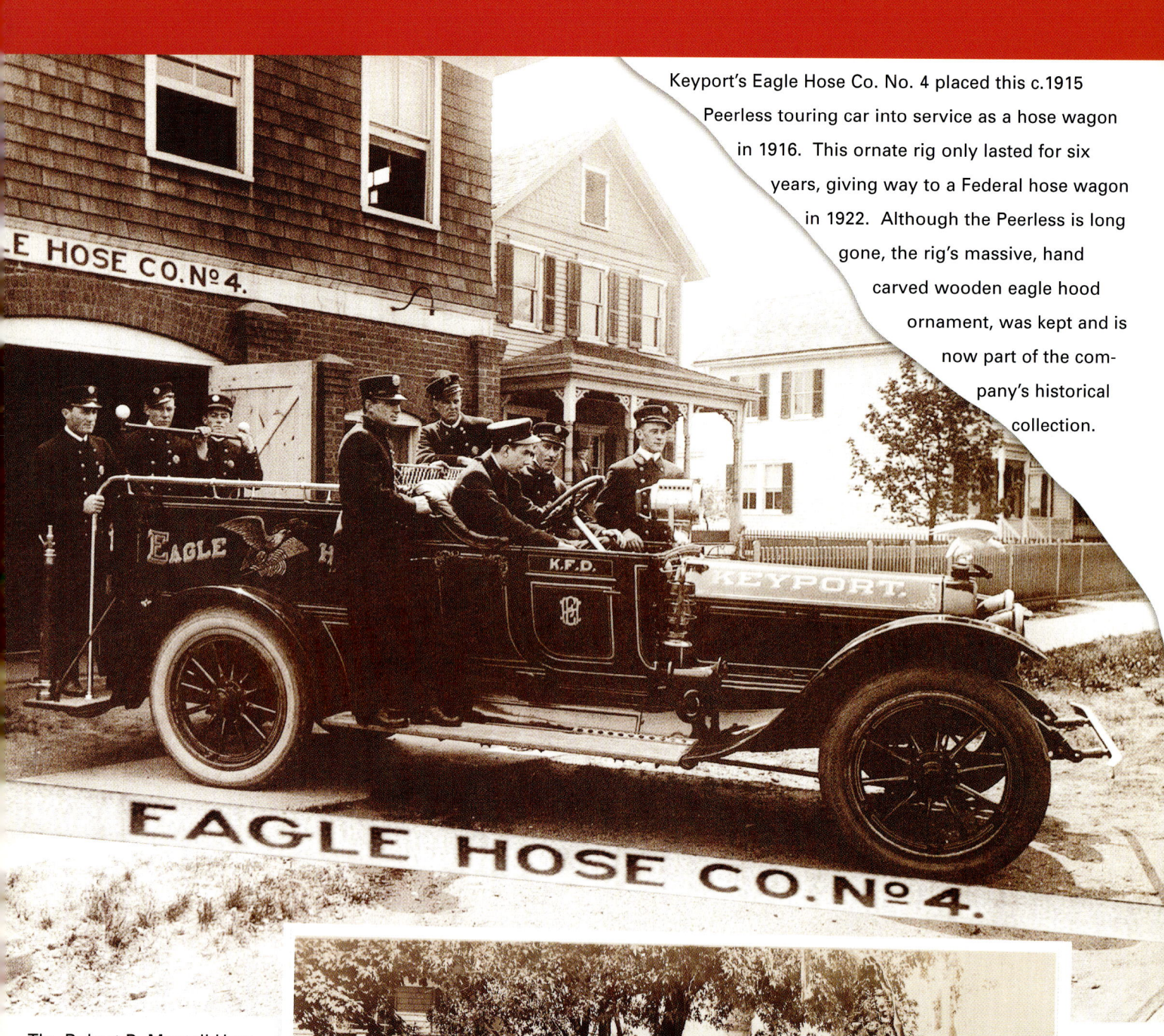

Keyport's Eagle Hose Co. No. 4 placed this c.1915 Peerless touring car into service as a hose wagon in 1916. This ornate rig only lasted for six years, giving way to a Federal hose wagon in 1922. Although the Peerless is long gone, the rig's massive, hand carved wooden eagle hood ornament, was kept and is now part of the company's historical collection.

The Robert B. Mantell Hose Company of Atlantic Highlands operated this 1916 hose wagon. This apparatus was the first motorized unit in the Atlantic Highlands Fire Department and served until 1931. The maker of this heavy duty car chassis remains a mystery.

08 Jersey Shore Fire Apparatus Volume 1 "Classics thru the 60's"

Delivered in 1919 to Long Branch's Independent Engine & Truck No. 2, this city service truck was built on a Mack AC chassis. This style of Mack was better known as the "Bulldog' Mack, named during World War I. By the time this photo was taken the rig had been retrofitted with pneumatic tires and a windshield. The design on the front hood is I M, which were the initials of the International Motor Co., Macks parent company of the time. This rig was eventually purchased by the Oceanport Hook & Ladder Company who operated it for many years after it left Long Branch.

This classy looking rig was once seen on the city streets in Long Branch. Serving the City for a long thirty-three years, it was purchased in 1922 from the International Motor Corporation. This Mack model AB did not have a water pump, however, carried a small chemical tank. It was operated by the city's Neptune Hose Co. No.1, organized in 1877.

The small Borough of Englishtown purchased this Seagrave pumper around 1928. This good looking rig was responsible for protecting such buildings as the Village Inn, which was used as General Washington's office during the battle of Monmouth.

What ? A Mack bulldog on a Seagrave city service truck? Manasquan Hook & Ladder Company was the proud owner of this 1927 model, which had a rather unusual looking windshield added in the late 1930's.

Belmar's Goodwill Fire Company had taken delivery of this Model A Ford hose wagon around 1928, just after Ford had introduced it. The little hose wagon is pictured here with its replacement 1940's vintage Seagrave Engine.

Two more of Belmar's Fire Company's took delivery of Seagrave products in the mid nineteen twenties, both vehicles were delivered in white. Only the Union Fire Co. would retain this color on future orders. While the Union ire Co. picked up this pumper (right), the V.H&LC received this sharp looking city service truck.

In 1926 The Stoughton Wagon Company, of Stoughton, Wisconsin manufactured this truck chassis on which Pirsch Fire apparatus added the body. Pirsch eventually bought the Stoughton Company and by the mid 1930's phased out this truck line. Union Beach Fire Company No. 1, better known as "White Company", operated this rig for many years from their old Union Avenue Firehouse.

In 1920, the Ocean Fire Company of Sea Bright took delivery of this American LaFrance. This apparatus appears to have not less than three lengths of hard suction for drafting from the Shrewsbury River.

This circa 1925 Mack AC was operated by Keansburg Borough Fire Company No. 1. The front fenders and windshield appear to be upgrades added at a later date along with the cowl mounted siren. The members were quite proud of her service record as can be seen by the large sign under the grille.

Jersey Shore Fire Apparatus Volume 1 "Classics thru the 60's" 11

American LaFrance registration #5993 was delivered to the Rumson Fire Company in 1927. This 1000-gpm job was eventually purchased by Middletown's newly formed Old Village Fire Company in December of 1955. Old Village kept the rig for many years, but finally sold it off in the 1980's.

Fire Protection in Long Branch first began with in 1866, when the Neptune Hook & Ladder Company was organized. Fifty-seven years later, the Elberon Engine Co. took delivery of this Aherns-Fox piston pumper. This unit served until the mid 1940's, and after engine problems it was sadly disposed of, being sold for a scrap metal drive during WWII.

Long Branch's Atlantic Engine & Truck Company decided on the New Jersey firm of Day-Elder to build this engine around 1927. Built in Irvington, this engine was equipped with a Continental gasoline engine and a 500-gpm pump. This photo was snapped along the Long Branch boardwalk in the 1950's.

The Oceanic Hook & Ladder Co. of Rumson operated this 1929 American LaFrance pumper. Bearing ALF reg. number #7162, it was housed for many years at the Rumson Volunteer Fire Co's station. It was later sold to its present owners, the East Freehold Fire Company.

Stutz Fire Apparatus were in their heyday when this delivery was made to West Long Branch Fire Co. 2 in 1922. From 1919 to 1928 the Stutz Fire Engine Company was located in Indianapolis, Indiana. They later went on to place the first diesel fire engine in service in the country in 1939. Although the WLBFD rig didn't come with a diesel her big Wisconsin engine coupled to a 500-gpm pump certainly did the job when called for.

Organized in 1911 as the John P.L. Tilton Chemical Fire Co. No. 1, members later decided to change the name to Hamilton Fire Co. In 1928 the Seagrave Corporation built this 500-gpm unit for the company. This rig's dark green, color stands alone on the roster, as all other apparatus in the company have been painted red.

The Wannamassa Fire Company was organized in 1922 to protect the rapidly growing community surrounding Deal Lake. By 1938 the company purchased this 1927 Stutz engine which had previously been operated by the Belmar Fire Department.

This classic photograph captures two Asbury Park apparatus while the department was still volunteer. This shot was taken at the current Headquarters building, which was home to the Allen R. Cook Chemical Company and the Neptune Hose Co.

This classic Aherns Fox model JM-4 was delivered to Deal Fire Company No. 2 in 1920. Sporting a 500-gpm pump, this rig was known as a pump, hose and booster car. Deal's Fox is outfitted with an array of running board mounted equipment such as Indian tanks, playpipes, nozzles and extinguishers.

Not much is known about this little rig which was delivered to the Asbury Park Fire Department around 1927. The chassis has been identified as a Martin, while the body was most likely built locally. Assigned to Neptune's Hose Co., this rig served until sometime around 1940.

Here is Farmingdale's Mack AB engine as it appeared shortly before it's delivery in 1924. This good looking rig has both a pump and a double tank chemical system. The Mack was the backbone of this small, rural borough for many, many years.

Jersey Shore Fire Apparatus Volume 1 "Classics thru the 60's"

One of three American LaFrance tillered aerials that served Monmouth County is shown here. Purchased in 1928 for the Eagle Hook & Ladder Co. of Ocean Grove, was this type 117 seventy five foot ladder. Note the full complement of wooden ground ladders. This company has operated as a two piece ladder company for many years.

CHAPTER II
1930 - 1950
The Classic Fire Engine

Many of the smaller rural fire companies only had one or two trucks, this photo of the Glendola Fire Company of Wall Township shows a circa 1935 Pirsch pumper and a 1946 Pirsch pumper.

Few Sealand Corp. Fire Apparatus were delivered in the Shore area. The Port Monmouth Fire Company of Middletown received this 1940 GMC Sealand pumper, that remained in service until 1988. Fair Haven, NJ also received a GMC Sealand but this one was built as patrol truck. The Sealand Corporation was based in Southport Conn.

Navesink Hook & Ladder Co No. 1 of Middletown Township operated this 1934 Seagrave 750-gpm pumper, until replaced by a 1960 Mack C 750-gpm pumper. This was the last truck whose mural included a Lenni Lenape Indian in full head dress. Since that time the Indian has sported a historically correct head dress with only two feathers.

The Stutz Fire Engine Company of Indianapolis Indiana, delivered this rig to the Brevent Park and Leonardo Fire Co. in 1936. It served the Bayshore area of Middletown Township until about 1970. In later years this rig saw duty as a brush truck during the spring and fall fire season.

Originally delivered to the East Keansburg Fire Company in white, this 1937 Diamond T/ Buffalo arrived with a 500-gpm pump. This unit was later repainted red, and was operated well into the 1970's by this company of the Middletown Fire Dept.

20 Jersey Shore Fire Apparatus Volume 1 "Classics thru the 60's"

Just before Christmas 1935, Good Will Hook & Ladder Co. of Freehold received this American LaFrance city service unit. This vehicle was responsible for all truck company duties in Western Monmouth County for many, many years. It served until 1963 when it was replaced by a new rig, this time an American LaFrance 900 series with an 85 foot aerial.

On April 24, 1948 the Monmouth Hose Company received this rugged looking Mack L engine. Equipped with 750-gpm this unit was the second motorized unit to serve in this Freehold Company. This style of Mack was rarely delivered with a enclosed cab in this area. It was replaced in 1970 with a new Mack CF engine.

The Goodwill Hook & Ladder of Freehold has always had some neat rigs. This 1941 Mack E served as an early attack truck for the county seat of Monmouth. It also perfomed duty on fires in Freehold Township in the days before housing developments. Goodwill provided fire protection to the township until the 1960's.

Jersey Shore Fire Apparatus Volume 1 "Classics thru the 60's"

This neat looking Sanford once served with Freewood Acres Fire Company in Howell township. This rig was purchased second hand by the company sometime in the 1950's. Freewood Acres is one of five fire Companies within Howell Township.

Located on Route 9 in Howell Township is the Southard Fire Company. Organized in 1933, the company took possession of this Ford/Ward LaFrance in 1947. In 1981, a Ford/Emergency One finally replaced this worn out rig.

Here is an interesting rig. The Adelphia Fire Company ordered this 500-gallon per minute Mack in 1941. But what is it? It is obviously built on a Mack E chassis but it has the windshield of and L model. Another one of Macks one off Friday odd part jobs. This rigs first major run was to the extensive Lakewood Forest Fires of 1941.

Jersey Shore Fire Apparatus Volume 1 "Classics thru the 60's"

After months of planning, the boy's of E.H. Stokes Fire Co. received this one of a kind Aherns-Fox HT pumper. Equipped with a 1000-gpm pump and a 100-gallon booster tank, this rig almost came in painted white, but the final vote was cast in favor of a more traditional red. All equipment on this rig was enclosed behind the streamlined body while the booster line was recessed into the rear step. It is currently owned by a local collector and is undergoing a complete restoration.

Located in Northern Monmouth County is Matawan's Midway Hose Company No. 2. Organized in 1903 this company took delivery of this Seagrave engine in 1940. This little rig saw plenty of action throughout Matawan and the surrounding areas until she was replaced in 1968 with a Maxim F model.

Jersey Shore Fire Apparatus Volume 1 "Classics thru the 60's"   23

Based on a Schacht truck Chassis this Ahrens-Fox 500-gpm centrifugal pumper was delivered to the Atlantic Township Fire Co. #1 in 1936. The Fox is shown parked on the ramp of the old firehouse located on Monmouth County Route 537. Unfortunately, this rig was destroyed in a barn fire.

Originally a fuel oil delivery truck, this very rare Dodge Airflow chassis provided the platform for a 1240 gallon locally built tanker in 1938. The rural Holmdel Fire Company acquired this truck from a local oil company and converted it into use as a fire department tanker during the 1950's. It is said by some old timers that, "this thing leaked like a siv".

This 1942 GMC/Buffalo was probably acquired from the US. Navy, and was one of the first trucks to be placed into service by Colts Neck Fire Co. No. 2. The naming of the township of Colts Neck (formerly Atlantic) has two origins, the first, it was named Cauls Neck after an early resident, the second and more interesting of the two, was that the renowned Race Horse, Old Fashioned, fell and broke its neck there.

24 Jersey Shore Fire Apparatus Volume 1 "Classics thru the 60's"

By the 1950's fire apparatus without pumps had become increasingly rare. Spring Lake's Fire Co. No. 1 took possession of this GMC hosewagon with bodywork by Seagrave in 1950. Although this was a modest piece of equipment the company still managed to adorn the vehicle with both chrome bumpers and grillwork along with a large bell mounted near the officer's side of the rig.

Photographed on the ramp of Brielle Fire House, is this 1949 General Motors Corp. truck with a Bean Hi-Pressure system. This rig was replaced during the 1970's. Since the late 1940's, many shore fire companies placed into service apparatus that were equipped with hi-pressure pumps. This unit had a 750-gpm pump and a high pressure pump.

Jersey Shore Fire Apparatus Volume 1 "Classics thru the 60's" 25

This 1934 Diamond T city service ladder truck served with the Keyport Hook & Ladder Co until 1958. The cost of this truck was $942.00 and was locally referred to as the "hay wagon". As one old timer put it when she first rolled into town, "That sure is nice hay wagon you got there".

Despite war time shortages of apparatus Keyport Engine Company No. 1 was able to replace their ancient 1919 American LaFrance chain driven engine with this Pump, Hose and Booster Car in 1941. The major differences between this style and the standard 600 series was that the cab was narrower, it had a V-wind-shield and the grille ended in a more vertical style near the fenders. This rig served until 1967.

This classic Mack L-80 was delivered to Keyport's Lincoln Hose Company in 1941. The rig contained a 750-gpm pump and a 300-gallon booster tank. It was repainted and relettered in 1953 after having been nearly destroyed in a lumberyard fire. In 1968, a new Mack CF took it's place in the firehouse, ending her proud twenty-seven years of service.

Deal Fire Company No. 2 used this this Mack Type 50 quadruple combination from 1940 until 1993. Equipped with a 500-gpm pump and a 200-gallon booster tank this rig proudly served the residents of Deal for many years. The cab on this Type 50 is a totally custom unit, like many of Macks designs in a time when custom built meant just that. Interestingly enough their is no longer a Deal Fire Company No. 1!

Jersey Shore Fire Apparatus Volume 1 "Classics thru the 60's"

Ocean Fire Company in Point Pleasant Beach has the disputed distinction of being the county's oldest fire company (Beach Haven was also organized in 1883). In 1949, this enclosed cab Ward LaFrance was received from the company's factory in Elmira Heights, New York. This rig has the standard Ward cowl mounted siren-light as well as three lengths of suction and a front suction, which was an unusual feature for a apparatus of this vintage.

Another Ward LaFrance operated by Point Pleasant Beach. This is a 1939 city service truck with a closed cab.

The Point Pleasant Beach Fire Company No. 2 also operated this handsome 1948 Ward LaFrance 1000-gpm pumper.

28 Jersey Shore Fire Apparatus Volume 1 "Classics thru the 60's"

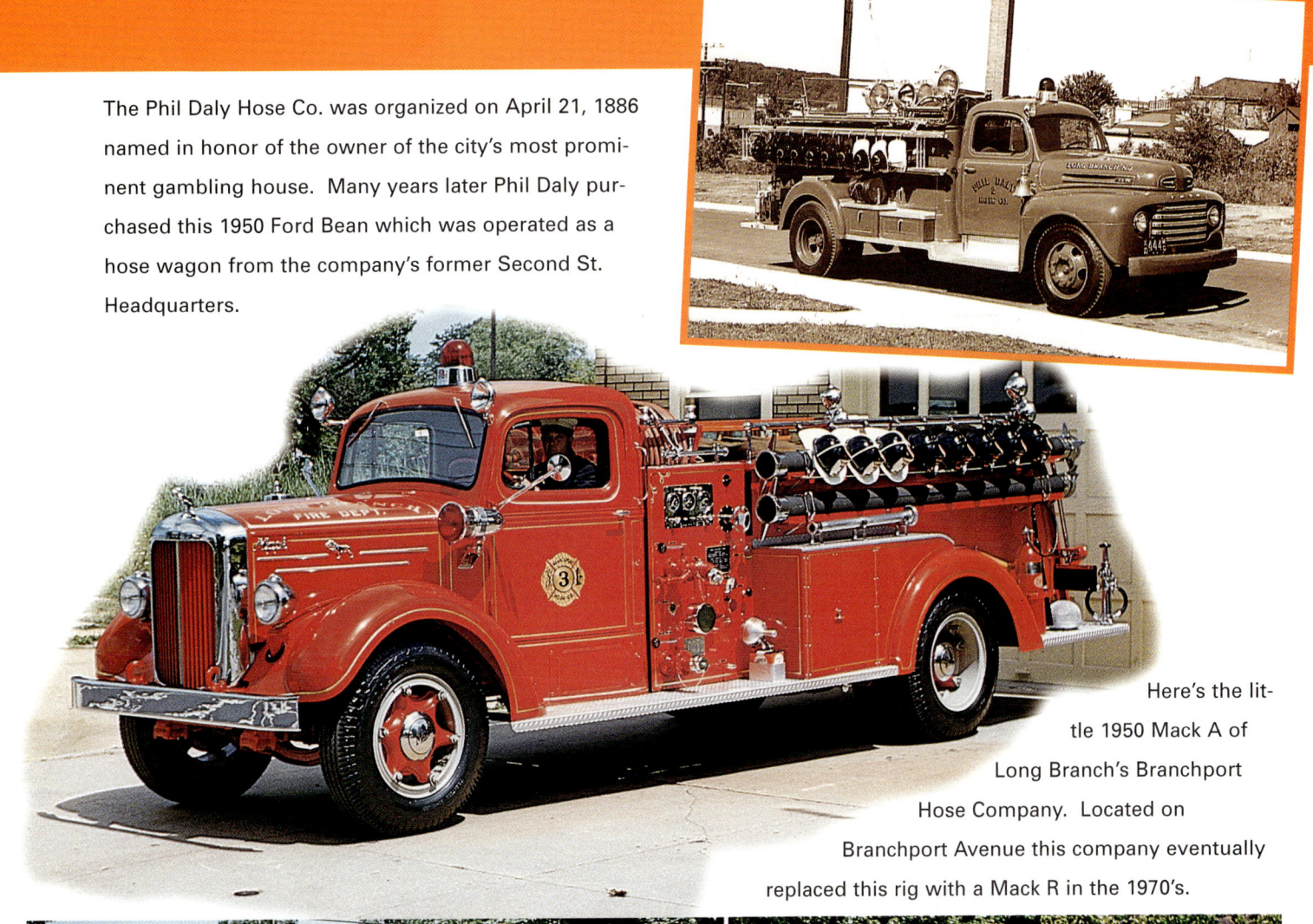

The Phil Daly Hose Co. was organized on April 21, 1886 named in honor of the owner of the city's most prominent gambling house. Many years later Phil Daly purchased this 1950 Ford Bean which was operated as a hose wagon from the company's former Second St. Headquarters.

Here's the little 1950 Mack A of Long Branch's Branchport Hose Company. Located on Branchport Avenue this company eventually replaced this rig with a Mack R in the 1970's.

This 1953 GMC had an early "paddy wagon" utility body. This interesting unit saw service with the Long Branch Fire Police Patrol. Many larger towns in the shore area began to organize separate fire patrols after the advent of the automobile, in an attempt to control the all too curious and sometimes hindering fire truck chasers of the day.

Jersey Shore Fire Apparatus Volume 1 "Classics thru the 60's"

The year 1946 saw the arrival of this Standard model Seagrave engine which was delivered to Goodwill Fire Co. of Belmar.

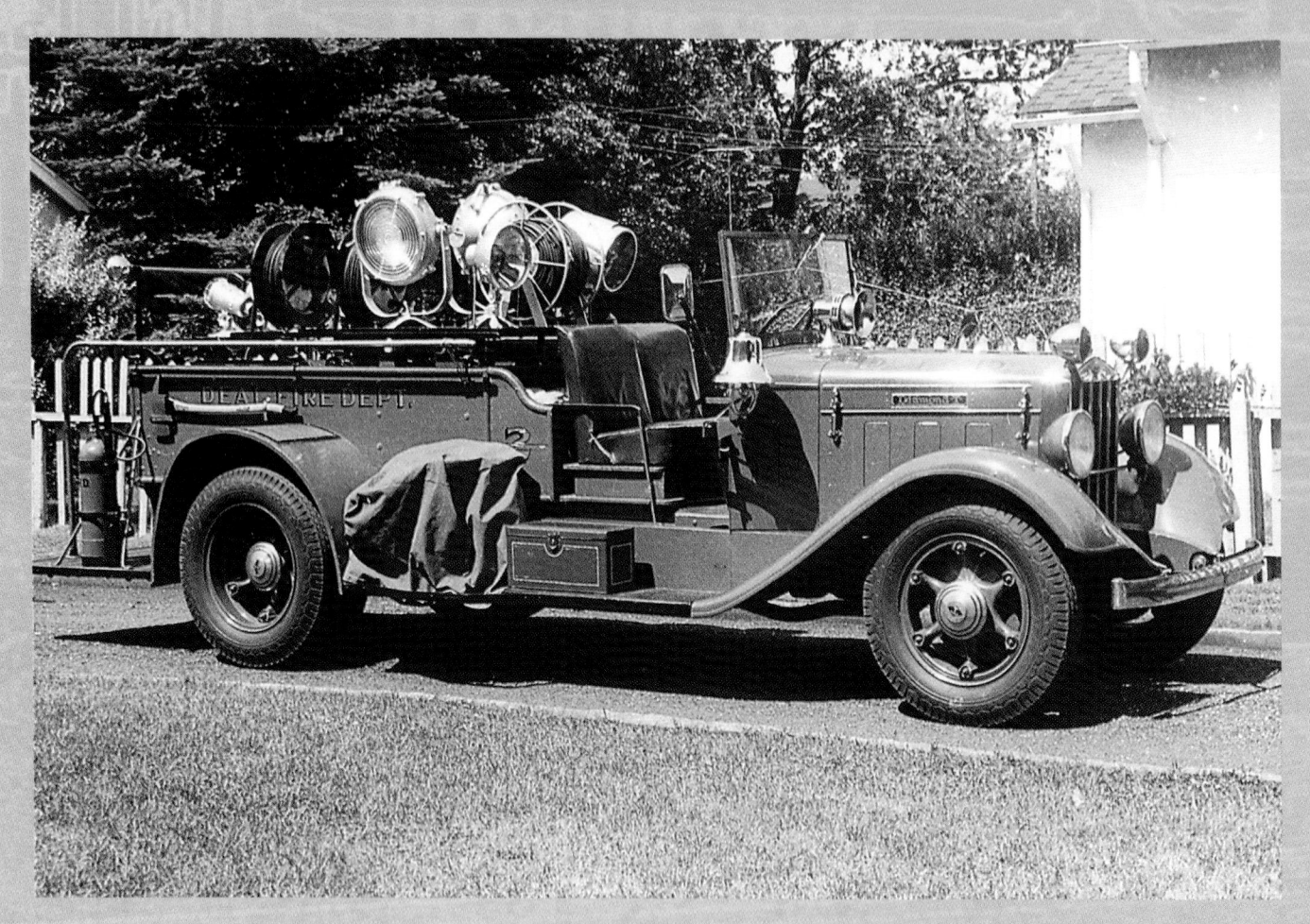

This small Diamond T floodlight unit was delivered to the Deal Fire Co. No. 2 in 1933. Company 2 was organized in 1912 to succeed Fire Co. No. 1 which has disbanded only two years after its formation in 1910 due to a dispute with towns governing body.

Volunteer Hook & ladder of Belmar once answered calls with this circa 1946 Seagrave sixty-five footer. Steel aerials were still a novelty in 1946, as many chiefs believed that only wooden ladders could do the job. This rig was finally replaced by a Hahn aerial in 1970, it also came with a steel aerial.

Morganville Independent Fire Company once ran these matching Mack type E-45 units. The pumper was a good looking 1940 model with a 500-gpm pump. Also housed in the Independent firehouse was this tanker which was an ex-fuel oil truck, from the same vintage. Both of these rigs have long since vanished from the Route 79 firehouse.

Jersey Shore Fire Apparatus Volume 1 "Classics thru the 60's"

Spring Lake Fire Co. # 1 operated this spartan looking 1947 American LaFrance 700 series pumper. 1947 marked the first year of production for the first true cab forward apparatus, which was a outgrowth of the American LaFrance JOX.

The Westside Hose Company in Red Bank was assigned this 750-gpm American LaFrance in 1947. It was one of three 700 series ALF's operated by the RBFD. This rig gave way in 1969 to a new American LaFrance 900 series pumper.

32 Jersey Shore Fire Apparatus Volume 1 "Classics thru the 60's"

Pirsch fire apparatus were seldom seen on the Jersey Shore, but Pirsch tillers are a real find. The City of Long Branch assigned this open-cab tiller to the Oceanic Engine & Truck Company in 1949. This rig was run out of the Norwood Avenue firehouse until replaced in 1974 by a Mack CF with a 100 foot Maxim ladder.

Rumson's Fire Department received this Federal searchlight and salvage car in 1933. The headlights were blacked out during World War II, to comply with civil defense rules. All shore communities had to take extreme measures to black out light to prevent enemy attack from both air and from U--Boats that were lurking off the coast.

Jersey Shore Fire Apparatus Volume 1 "Classics thru the 60's" 33

This Circa 1942 ex-military GMC crash truck was purchased by the Gordon's Corner Fire Company sometime in the early 1960's. It's origin is unknown, however, it appears to be a U.S. navy job. Note the extra large CO_2 horn mounted on the side of the running board. Although it is a little mysterious it certainly was an interesting looking rig!

Point Pleasant Boro Fire Co. No. 2 had this 1942 Chevy 4x4 ex military truck, which was equipped with a 300-gallon water tank. It served as their first fire apparatus. This chassis was extremely popular during World War II, with countless body types installed on these chassis.

Another chassis made famous by World War II, was the GMC CCKW, which was built by various General Motors factories throughout America. This 6x6 was converted into a brush fire unit by the Farmingdale Fire Company sometime in the 1950's. The unit was equipped with a 500-gpm pump and a 1000-gallon tank.

Parkertown Fire Company used this former WWII G7-107 1 1/2 ton cargo truck in the 1950's and 60's. Many former military trucks provided cheap, chassis well built for use as fire apparatus.

34 Jersey Shore Fire Apparatus Volume 1 "Classics thru the 60's"

Mack produced the small E model chassis from 1936-1951, as a choice between the larger L and A models. This circa 1947 was in service with the Shark River Hills Fire Company of Neptune Township.

Cliffwood Fire Company No. 1 purchased this Mack E pumper in 1941. Equipped with a 500-gpm pump and 300-gallon booster tank, this little rig was the first painted in the company's, now standard color of white. In service until 1963, it eventually made it's way to Wayside Fire Company of Tinton Falls where she was repainted red and served for several more years.

A Mack E was the choice of Neptune's Unexcelled Fire Company in 1942. Most likely able to pump 750-gpm, this rig served until 1971 when it was replaced with a Hahn engine.

Neptune City's fire company is known as the United Fire Company. This workhorse was built by Mack on an E Style chassis, and ran with a 500-gallon pump. Summer traffic must have been a breeze to clear out with both a cowl mounted siren and a roof mounted siren. The Unexcelled Fire Co. in nearby Neptune Twp. ran a similar closed-cab rig.

Jersey Shore Fire Apparatus Volume 1 "Classics thru the 60's" 35

Engine No. 2 of the Asbury Park Fire Department operated this 500 series ALF starting in 1939. This department which was originally volunteer became Monmouth County's only fully paid municipal fire department.

Oceanic Engine & Truck Co. of Long Branch operated this 500 Series American LaFrance. Delivered in 1939 the 500 series would soon be replaced by the 700 series after the war.

The Borough of Eatontown was protected by the Engine, Truck & Hose Co. No. 1. First motorized in 1917, the department received this American LaFrance series 500 in 1946. It served until c. 1968 when it was purchased by the Lanoka Harbor Fire Co. in Ocean County.

Just before World War II began, the Highland's Fire Department received this 500 series American LaFrance pumper. Operated by the Columbus Hose Company, this engine had the standard features such as the streamlined overhead ladder rack and the pump panel controls located on the right handside. American LaFrance had introduced this totally new design in June of 1940.

Here is East Dover's 1940 Seagrave 750-gpm pumper just waiting for that big call to come in. This semi-open-cab job is equipped with a cowl mounted oscillating light and three forward facing flashers. The center mounting of the siren-light is typical of American LaFrances during this time period. Note the absence of the turret pipe.

The tiny Borough of Allenhurst took delivery of this fine looking Seagrave 65-ft aerial ladder in 1950. Capable of pumping 500-gallons per minute this rig was the pride and joy of the Allenhurst Boy's until 1984, when it's long overdue replacement, a Seagrave 100-ft rear-mount arrived in the firehouse and took her place.

Bradley Beach's Pioneer Fire Co. No. 1 received this 1939 Seagrave Full Grill style Quad, complete with pump, hose, ladders and a booster tank. Originally delivered in white, it was later painted red. It was replaced by a GMC/ Seagrave aerial in the 1960's.

Jersey Shore Fire Apparatus Volume 1 "Classics thru the 60's"

Mack had a reputation for producing one-off custom jobs and this 1949 quadruple combination is a prime example. Delivered to the Independent Hose Co. of the Oakhurst section of Ocean Twsp., this nice looking rig was later sold to the Harris Gardens Fire Co. in Union Beach during the 1970's. It later came to rest behind a car wash where it sat for many years before disappearing into the history books.

Purchased just nine years after their organization, the Lincroft Fire Co. received this White pumper in 1949. The total cost of the new rig was $3800 and was delivered by Ernie Day's firm of New Jersey Fire Equipment.

Freewood Acres Fire Company is the newest of five companies in Howell Township. Started in the mid 1950's, one of the company's first trucks was this homemade 1940's vintage Ford. The truck was equipped with a front-mount pump, booster equipment and over head ladder rack.

A classic example of a Ward LaFrance pumper is this 1940 job for Englishtown. This unit was built in a very streamlined style, with fender skirts, torpedo headlights, and a transverse gear rack.

Ocean County's Seat of Toms River took delivery of this long American LaFrance quad in 1936. This rig was a favorite at parades with a chrome double bumper, siren and large floodlights. It remained on the company's roster well into the 1960's.

Monmouth Beach received this large American LaFrance pumper in 1930. This rig served until 1964, when it was replaced by a Hahn Quad. Monmouth Beaches' first ALF was a 1920 model.

Hazlet Fire Company ordered this long wheelbase TASC pumper on a 1949 International KB chassis. After being replaced in 1975, it sat rusting away in a field around the corner from the firehouse for many years. It disappeared by 1991.

The M.E. Haley Hose Company of Matawan also received this new 1943 pumper. It had a sleek enclosed-cab Diamond T. This rig was assembled by Ward LaFrance and looked mighty sporty with flared fenders, rear wheelskirts and monochrome trim. This rig served for only seven years when it was replaced with a new custom 1950 Ward LaFrance engine (with an open-cab!).

G.M.C.s' snub nosed COE model was used for relatively few fire apparatus chassis. Highland's Star Hook & Ladder Company must have been overwhelmed by the beauty of this chassis, and was compelled to mount the body of their 1920 Mack city service truck on this one in 1950. This rig is lettered for No. 6 of the H.F.D.. Note the visible absence of a siren and bell.

One of the first and only companies that operated a ladder truck in Southern Ocean County was the Beach Haven Vol. Fire Co. on Long Beach Island. The company had used this 1949 American LaFrance Quad.

A custom "Clear Vision" Buffalo pumper was delivered in 1945 to the South Belmar Fire Department. This 750-gpm pumper had a streamlined body which housed the equipment that was carried. The lack of chrome suggested that this unit was delivered before the close of WWII.

Here's something a little different. This used 1939 Chevy Sedan delivery was purchased during WWII for the Auxiliary Fire Department of Long Branch. Complete with a front mount pump and overhead ladder rack, this unit's European look was reminiscent of the "fire appliances" that were pressed into service by Britain's Auxiliary Fire Service during the blitz attacks of 1941.

The New Egypt Fire Company in Plumstead Twsp. once operated this 1949 Pirsch custom pumper. Most likely equipped with 500-gpm pump, this rig is shown on the apron of the company's second firehouse which was built in the 1950's.

Jersey Shore Fire Apparatus Volume 1 "Classics thru the 60's" 43

Few Sanfords were delivered in this period however, this one made its way to here during 1935. The Northside Engine Company was located in new Shrewsbury which later became part of Tinton Falls.

Manitou Park Fire Company kept this 1940's vintage Dodge on the roster until the 1990's when the aging unit was disposed of.

The Beachwood Fire Company received this Diamond T Pirsch in 1937. A 500-gpm pump was mounted on this rig while a 350-gallon booster tank provided the water supply.

The first fire company in Ocean Township was the Oakhurst Ind. Hose Co. They used this small 1947 IHC / Approved pumper.

Seaside Park, located just south of Seaside Heights, once operated this custom Oren 750-gpm pumper. This unit only had a 275-gallon water tank.

This 1947 Ford was equipped with a John Bean Hi-Pressure Fog System. It was on the roster of Manasquan's Hook & Ladder Company for many years. It's replacement was also a Ford, this time on a C style chassis and also with a Bean Hi-Pressure system.

The Methodist meeting camp of Ocean Grove received this 1929 Maccar hose wagon, and placed it into service with the E.H. Stokes Fire Co. The body was fabricated by the Adam Black Body Company of Jersey City. This unit carried 1000-ft of 2-1/2 inch hose, and also sported a fire boat style deluge gun capable of flowing 1200-gpm. The Maccar was replaced in 1959 and went on to serve as the fire police truck for the Borough of Bradley Beach.

Pine Brook, located in Tinton Falls, organized their own fire company in the 1940's. This 1947 International/Approved 500-gpm pumper served this company for many years.

This former oil tanker was purchased by Jackson Mills Fire Co. during the 1950's. It is a 1940 GMC which held approximate 1100 gallons of water.

In 1947 the West Long Branch Fire Company No. 1 received this rather large Hahn pumper. It is one of the few Hahns of this style to have served in the shore area.

46 Jersey Shore Fire Apparatus Volume 1 "Classics thru the 60's"

Adelphia once shuttled water from their Rt. 524 firehouse with this tanker. The trailer of this tanker was pulled by a '49 White COE. It was one of the first tractor drawn tankers in the area.

The oldest fire company in Monmouth County operated this unusual 1953 Ford pumper which had a 500-gpm front mounted pump. Allentown's Hope Fire Company which was organized in 1850, chose a local builder to complete the body on this pumper.

In June 1967 the East Freehold Fire Company was organized to protect the Eastern part of Freehold Township. They began with several used apparatus. Among them was this 1956 GMC/TASC that carried a 750-gpm pump and a 750-gallon tank.

Jersey Shore Fire Apparatus Volume 1 "Classics thru the 60's" 47

Chapter III
1951 - 1965
Cab Overs, Diesels and the Modern Era

The Seagrave Sedan style pumper was developed in 1936 for the Detroit Fire Department. Few of these rigs were delivered anywhere else. Two were known to be delivered in New Jersey, one for Tenafly which is still owned by that department, and the second a 1952 750-gpm pumper delivered to the Robert B. Mantell Hose Co. #2 of Atlantic Highlands. This unit was equipped with a rear facing bench seat with a fully enclosed hose body, and a 500-gallon tank. This rig was always an eye catcher and a welcome site during parades.

One of the last 700 series American LaFrances to be delivered was this 1956 model, which went to the Freehold Fire Department. Assigned to Engine & Hose Co. No. 1, this was the company's first closed-cab apparatus. It was replaced in 1977 by a Century Series ALF.

The Squankum Fire Co. of Howell Townships first fire truck was this home made 1946 Chevy Tanker. The front-mounted pump and over head ladder were added to this 1000-gallon tanker by the members.

Red Bank's Relief Fire Company took advantage of American LaFrance's best selling fire apparatus chassis, which was delivered in 1951. Complete with a 1000-gpm pump, a siren-light and front suction, this classic rig served until 1972 at which time it was replaced by another American LaFrance.

Jersey Shore Fire Apparatus Volume 1 "Classics thru the 60's"

Rumson Fire Company #1 received this 1952 American LaFrance 700 series pumper equipped with a 1000-gpm pump. In 1982, a Hahn HCP replaced this aging classic.

Wayside Community Fire Company in Tinton Falls (then known as New Shrewsbury) operated this 1950 Ford F-8. The H & H Body company of Jersey City constructed this unit with a 500-gpm high pressure pump and a rather large 800-gallon tank. Tinton Falls Fire Company No.1 operated a very similar rig during this time.

The North Side Engine Company of New Shrewsburg, now called Tinton Falls. This is a 1960 Ford F-800/ Great Eastern 750-gpm pumper was donated to the Lanton Volunteer Fire Department, of West Plains, MO. This was reported as their newest truck, on the day this book went to the printer. The Spring Lake Fore Co #1. and the Wayside Fire Company of Tinton Falls, also donated old apparatus to the volunteer of the Lanton Fire Dept.

Designated Engine No. 3 of the Lakehurst Fire Department, this Ward LaFrance 750-gpm pumper arrived in 1954. During the early 1950's, Ward LaFrance was building two distinct models of apparatus which could be easily distinguished by the height of the rig's windshields.

United Fire Co of Neptune City also received this early Ford C utility truck. Many shore town ran utility trucks, which were only rigs equipped with a generator and flood lights. This truck was replaced in 1977 by another Ford C/ saulsbury utility rescue unit.

Carrying 750-gallons of water in her booster tank this 1953 Ward LaFrance also sported a 750-high pressure pump. Mantaloking's rig was a progressive pumper of the day, this good looking rig had a Federal Q siren mounted the typical WLF way, as well as triple suctions and coat and boot rails.

Jersey Shore Fire Apparatus Volume 1 "Classics thru the 60's"   51

Laurelton Fire Company of Brick Townships operated this "business only" Ward LaFrance for many years. Delivered in 1958 it had a 750-pump and a large 1500-gallon booster tank.

Middletown's Fire Department is comprised of eleven fire companies which have stations throughout the different sections of the township. The Belford section is the location of two fire companies; Belford Engine Co. and Independent Fire Co. The Independent Fire Company received the first quint in the area during 1958 with the delivery of this 800 series 75-foot ALF.

This rather odd looking 1952 International L / Approved pumper stayed in service with the River Plaza Hose Co. of Middletown until 1982. This style of chassis was uncommon in the Northeast, but was widely operated in the Western States.

52 Jersey Shore Fire Apparatus Volume 1 "Classics thru the 60's"

Most fire apparatus are known by big burly manly man names, however this little piece is more likely to be considered just plain "cute". Built on a 1954 Chevy chassis, this pick-up was turned into a very early miniature - pumper. Complete with a 250-gpm pump and 2-1/2 hard suction and it served until 1989.

The Township of Lakewood in Ocean County operates a combination career and volunteer fire department from a total of seven stations. During the 1960's the sole paid firefighter operated this 1960 International 250-gpm unit. Complete with a front mounted pump, high pressure booster lines and small aerial ladder this rig could pack quite a powerful punch.

Cliffwood Fire Company of Matawan (Aberdeen) Township, took delivery of this 1964 Dodge W-300 Power Wagon / American LaFrance crash truck. Reportedly the company was searching for a brush truck, and their long time American LaFrance salesman knew of this Little-Mo crash truck. The price of the unit was right and so this 250 gpm pumper arrived at the Angel Street Firehouse where it served until 1982.

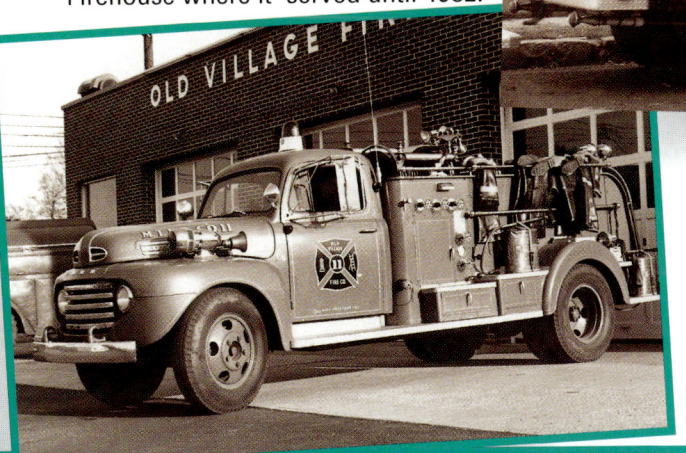

This circa 1949 Ford/Bean High Pressure Fog unit was in service with the Old Village Fire Company No. 11 of Middletown Township. This rigs early life is unknown as the Old Village Company was started in the mid 1950's. After serving Company 11, this unit was put into service with the East Freehold Fire Company.

Jersey Shore Fire Apparatus Volume 1 "Classics thru the 60's"   53

For many, fire engines should be red, but don't dare tell the firefighters in Brick Township's Breton Woods Fire Company. One of the many good looking green rigs operated by this company was this 1959 B model Mack which had a 1000-gpm pump and a large 1000-gallon booster tank.

After a large Forest Fire in 1963, served men in Western Freehold Township, started the Freehold Township Independent Fire Company. For the next several years, the company used donated, or bought old fire apparatus from local fire companies. This 1952 Ford/Great Eastern had a 500-gpm pump and 600-gallon tank. It was taken out of service in the mid 1970's.

The Hamilton Fire Company operated this 1957 Mack B model. Complete with a closed cab and 750-gpm pump this rig was a real workhorse in its day.

Unexcelled Fire Company in Neptune operated this 1958 American LaFrance 700 series ladder until 1981. It was then replaced by a 100-ft American LaFrance Ladder Chief. This 75-ft. steel aerial unit came equipped with a booster pump and a 300-gallon tank. After leaving Neptune it served with the West Long Branch Fire Co. No. 2 until 1991.

American Lafrance unveiled their new 900 series in mid 1958. This totally redesigned apparatus featured vast improvement from the 700/800 which had been in production since 1947. The Unexcelled Fire Co. picked up this 750-gpm a 900 the same year it debuted. They were very pleased with this one they purchased another 900 series in 1963.

This rare custom Oren pumper was once the pride and joy of the Community Fire Co. in the Leonardo section of Middletown Twp. Its long career lasted until 1982 when it was removed from active duty and then assigned to the Township's Fire Academy.

Jersey Shore Fire Apparatus Volume 1 "Classics thru the 60's"

Bradley Beach had two classic cab-over GMC/Seagrave units. This rather interesting looking 1963 GMC/Seagrave 75-ft aerial was once run by the Borough's Pioneer Fire Company. All three of Bradley Beach's Fire Company's were dissolved circa 1989 at which time the Bradley, Pioneer and Independent Fire Co's became simply the Bradley Beach Fire Department.

Howell's Southard Fire Company was once the owner of this mid 1950's Ford Ward LaFrance 750-gpm pumper.

This "Emergency Unit" was operated by the Liberty Fire Company which was originally organized in 1905 to protect the Whitesville section of Neptune Township. Built on an International L series chassis circa 1951, this unit's body was completed by an unknown builder.

56 Jersey Shore Fire Apparatus Volume 1 "Classics thru the 60's"

Seaside Heights specified Pirsch as the builder of their new ladder truck in 1959. Equipped with a 75-ft steel ladder this good looking rig had the later style boxed fenders which first appeared Circa 1957.

Coastal towns were sometimes found to buy small pumpers to maneuver the older streets. The Independent Company No. 2 of Bradley Beach received this 1957 GMC/Seagrave 500 gpm pumper. This unit had a 500-gallon booster tank.

ISLAND HEIGHTS

Island Heights Fire Company, provides fire protection to the small town that is surrounded by Dover Township. This small fire company used this 1976 GMC cab-over TASC Pumper.

Jersey Shore Fire Apparatus Volume 1 "Classics thru the 60's" 57

In 1959 American LaFrance debuted their new cab forward design. The 900 series proved to be a very successful design remaining in production until 1970. The Sea Bright Fire Department is a long time user of American LaFrance Products. This 1963 American LaFrance 750-gpm pumper with a 500-gallon tank served into the early 1990's.

This 1958 FWD once served the Ocean Township community of Wanamassa. Later, it was placed into service with the Wayside Community Fire Company of New Shrewsbury (now known as Tinton Falls.) Fitted with a 1000 gallon per minute pump and 1000 gallon booster tank this rig could launch a formidable attack on any size fire.

A rather rare manufacturer to serve the Jersey Shore was this General Detroit. This 1954 GMC/ 750-gpm pumper had a 500-gallon tank. This unit was purchased through the Civil Defense program for the Sea Bright Fire Department.

Point Pleasant Borough's first aerial ladder was this 1966 Ford C tractor. It was mated to a 1928 American LaFrance wooden tiller, which had formerly served the Eagle Hook & Ladder Company of Ocean Grove.

A long time customer of Hahn apparatus, Point Pleasant Borough Fire Company No. 1 also received this GMC cab-over with Hahn bodywork in 1962. This unit had a large 1000-gallon booster tank and was rated at 750-gpm.

The Avon By The Sea Fire Department ran two Great Easterns. One of which is this attractive 1957 Ford Great Eastern 750-gpm pumper. This unit was replaced by a Hahn HCP pumper in 1979.

Elberon Engine Company No. 4 of Long Branch used this tough looking 1963 FWD 1000-gpm pumper until it was replaced by another FWD in 1986.

The tiny borough of Roosevelt, located in Western Monmouth County was originally known as Jersey Homesteads. This 1960 FWD, formerly served the Richardson Engine Company of Freehold until 1982. It was the only engine of the Roosevelt Fire Department. This rig had a 1000-gpm pump and a 300-gallon tank.

Cincinnati cabs began to appear at the shore in the early 1960's. One of the first was this 1962 FWD 1000-gpm pumper. This cream colored unit served the Wanamassa Fire Company in Ocean Township in Monmouth County.

One of the first Cincinnati cabs in the bayshore area was this custom Hahn 1000-gpm pumper. Delivered to the Hazlet Fire Company, it was the first of four Hahns that would eventually be purchased. It served until being replaced by a new Hahn in 1988.

62 Jersey Shore Fire Apparatus Volume 1 "Classics thru the 60's"

This rather tough looking 1960 GMC tandem pumper-tanker was in service with the Whiting Fire Co. of Manchester Township. The body was built by TASC, and was equipped with a 750-gpm pump and 2000-gallon tank.

Many communities along the shore operated tankers due to limited municipal water supplies. Lakewood Engine Co. No. 1 operated this straight tanker. This unit is a rarity, first the chassis is an odd 1957 Dodge, and secondly the body was built by the Jersey City firm of H&H. This is the only tanker built by H&H. This unit served until 1982.

Manalapan Township has two companies, this one, officially the Manalapan Fire Company, is commonly referred to as the Millhurst Fire Company. Millhurst operated this 1963 International R Series/Hahn pumper-tanker, with an unusual 750-gpm front-mounted pump. This "Western" style apparatus carried 2000-gallons of water, and was replaced in 1989.

Jersey Shore Fire Apparatus Volume 1 "Classics thru the 60's" 63

Originally serving the City of Elizabeth, this 1958 Diamond T tractor was purchased by the city to modernize a 1928 Seagrave wooden tiller. After being placed out of service in Elizabeth, the Breton Woods Fire Company purchased this kitbashed rig and quickly repainted the rig forest green. After many years of service, this tractor-drawn job was sold off to a collector in North Jersey.

Lakewood Hook & Ladder Co. still has this 1955 Mack B/Maxim 75ft ladder in service. This unit came equipped with a 250-gpm pump and a 150-gallon tank. Ladder 465 is second due truck in the township of Lakewood.

Refurbished in 1984 by Middleboro Motors, this 1959 Maxim was originally delivered with an open-cab to the Toms River Fire Co. No. 1. This sharp looking 75-ft ladder served as the second piece of the ladder company until the 1990's when it was finally sold.

Jersey Shore Fire Apparatus Volume 1 "Classics thru the 60's"

This late 1950's International S chassis was built as a 1200-gallon tanker equipped with a front-mounted pump. The body builder on this rig is unknown, but was in service with the Jackson Volunteer Fire Company No. 1 as recently as 1988.

The Shrewsbury Hose Company operated this 1956 Ward LaFrance 750-gpm pumper, that held 500-gallons of water until 1992

Jackson Mills Fire Company operated this military M-37 vehicle as a brush unit for several years.

Jersey Shore Fire Apparatus Volume 1 "Classics thru the 60's"

One of the more confusing names for a fire company in the area is the Aberdeen Hose & Chemical Co. No. 1. Known as the Matawan Hose & Chemical Co. until 1981, the company has always been referred to as Oak Shades, which was the section of Matawan Twp. in which they were formed. This 1955 Ford/Great Eastern (Oren) was equipped with a 750-gpm pump and a rather large 850-gallon tank.

In 1954 a local resident donated a much needed Chevy tanker to the Middletown Fire Co. No 1 until the company could raise funds for the purchase of a newer rig. 1959 saw the delivery of a Mack B chassis on which the old tank was then mated to. This tandem rig was one of three Mack B's which made up this companies fleet. The other two included a pumper and a quad.

Here's a real eye catcher. This 1962 GMC/H&H 65ft quint, was built utilizing a Grove aerial ladder. Complete with chrome fender flares and gadgets galore this ladder served with the Shrewsbury Hose Company until the early 1990's.

Ward LaFrance introduced their first cab-over apparatus in 1962. Designated the Firebrand, it could seat two in the front and five along a rear facing bench seat. This Firebrand was purchased in 1963 by the Freewood Acres Fire Company and contained a 750-gpm John Bean Hi - Pressure pump as well as a 750-gallon water tank.

One of the most progressive deliveries of the 1960's this 1965 Seagrave K model pumper. Delivered with a 1500-gpm pump to the Liberty Hose Company of Red Bank, this rig served until 1986 when it was replaced by another 1500-gpm Seagrave. Liberty Hose has always been ahead of progress and this Seagrave was no exception.

Jersey Shore Fire Apparatus Volume 1 "Classics thru the 60's"

Built by the American LaFrance Corp., for the Ocean Grove Fire Department, this hose wagon was mounted on a 1959 GMC chassis. This unit had a 250-gallon booster pump and 300-gallon tank. Innovative for it's time it also had a 1500-watt generator and a portable deck gun.

Several shore fire departments operated hose wagons. This 1965 International Loadstar/TASC hose wagon sported a 200-gpm pump and a 500-gallon tank. It was used as the second piece to the Washington Fire Company of Ocean Grove.

One of the the few two piece truck companies along the shore is the Eagle Hook & Ladder Company of Ocean Grove. This 1956 Seagrave 70th Anniversary City Service Truck served as part of a two price truck company.

68 Jersey Shore Fire Apparatus Volume 1 "Classics thru the 60's"

The Naval Ammunition Depot Earle once shuttled water with this circa 1952 Autocar tanker. Equipped with a diesel engine, this rig had a big job to do hauling 3000-gallons of water around to protect our country's ships and sailors.

For may years the Freneau Fire Company of Matawan was an Independent Fire Company. Named in honor of Phillip Freneau the Revolutionary Poet , the company operated this 1959 Chevy COE tractor which pulled an older style tank trailer. Later this company became part of the Matawan Borough Fire Dept. and the tanker disappeared with the advent of hydrants.

Many shore communities relied on tankers to act as their water supply system. Lanoka Harbor Fire Company in Lacey Township operated this 1953 International R tractor drawn tanker with a unknown type trailer. Total water in this big rig was 5000 gallons.

One of three fire companies in Lacey Township, the Forked River Fire Company, operated this 1954 Oren 1000-gpm pumper that came delivered with a 1000-gallon tank.

This post World War II Mack L pumper served the Manchester Fire Company in Ocean County. Manchester's rig has all sort's of equipment mounted on this workhorse, including floodlights, Indian Tanks, three lengths of suction and a post mounted roto-ray way up front.

Pleasant Plains Fire Company of Dover Township operated this 1950's Ward Lafrance pumper.

During the 1960's brush trucks were just beginning to make their appearance in the area. North Centerville Fire Company of Hazlet Township needed a brush truck to fit down some narrow trails. They purchased a 1961 Willys Jeep and had it outfitted with a small pump and a 100-gallon booster tank. This unit served until another 1982 when another Jeep, this one a refined CJ5 replaced it.

Oceanport's Hook & Ladder Company used this 1952 Mack L, 750-gpm pumper until 1969 when it was replaced by a Mack CF. This attractive looking rig had a 300-gallon booster tank.

Trautwein and Sons Company originally built fire truck bodies in Woodbridge, after approximately 40 years and 250 trucks, the company ceased production of custom fire apparatus. This 1962 GMC/TASC 500-gpm pumper served the Manitou Park Fire Company of Berkeley Township.

Jersey Shore Fire Apparatus Volume 1 "Classics thru the 60's"

By the mid 1950's many communities had begun to rely upon the awesome water carrying power of tractor drawn tankers. Independent Fire Company of Morganville mated this 1957 Mack B tractor with a 40's vintage tank trailer in the early 1960's. This rig was quite a site screaming up and down the hills of Marlboro Township with it's 5000 gallons of water in tow. This trailer was originally towed by a circa 1954 Ford COE.

This brute of a tanker was operated by the East Freehold Fire Company during the 1960's and 70's. Built on a 1958 Chevy, the tractor had been donated by Brock Farms while the 6000-gallon tanker was a gift from a local oil company.

72 Jersey Shore Fire Apparatus Volume 1 "Classics thru the 60's"

Located on the "Island", the Ocean Beach Fire Co. of Dover Township placed this Ford/Oren pumper in service in 1950.

Belmar's Volunteer Hook & Ladder Company once operated this 1961 GMC utility and salvage unit. After being replaced in 1983, this rig was given to the First Aid Squad who operated it as a crash truck.

Very similar to Pine Beach's rig, this GMC pumper of Barnegat, was also built by TASC of Woodbridge during 1954. It was operated until the mid 1990's when it was finally retired from service.

Trautwein and Sons of Woodbridge turned out this mid size GMC pumper for the Borough of Pine Beach, NJ in 1953. It was equipped with a 750-gallon pump and a 750-gallon tank and was replaced in the early 1990's

Jersey Shore Fire Apparatus Volume 1 "Classics thru the 60's" 73

Manasquan Engine Co. No.2 has had a few antiques in their station, among them, a 1922 American LaFrance pumper and this 1960 Approved pumper, equipped with a 750-gpm pump and a 500-gallon tank. The cab is the same design as the unforgettable Mack C, which was an original design of the Ahrens Fox Corporation, Mack received the rights to this style cab after their 1958 take over of Ahrens-Fox. Another similar Approved unit was received by the New Point Comfort Fire Company of Keansburg.

In 1998 the Spring Lake Heights Independent Fire Company, replaced this well kept 1964 Maxim S 1000 gpm-pumper. This open cab unit had a 300-gallon booster tank. Few conventional Maxim apparatus were delivered during this era, as the new "Cab-Over" designs were quickly winning the hearts of firefighters everywhere.

Many fire companies in Central and South Jersey have brush trucks. One of the most common models was the Dodge Power Wagons. Many brush trucks were built to the NJ Forest Fire Service's design. This mid 1960's Forest Fire Service Dodge W-300 had a 200-gpm pump and a 250-gallon water tank.

This conventional GMC with a Great Eastern body was delivered to the Glendola Fire Co. circa 1960. It came equipped with a 750-gpm pump. Concerning Great Eastern Fire Apparatus- Mr. Ernie Day was the top seller of Oren Fire Trucks, therefore he received rights to sell Orens under his own brand name of Great Eastern.

74 Jersey Shore Fire Apparatus Volume 1 "Classics thru the 60's"

Chapter IV
The Survivors
Those who escaped the scrapyard

Known officially as the Skirmisher model, the "Four Way Combination" or to many, simply as a quad, was this 1928 Aherns-Fox. It has been owned by the Island Heights Fire Company in Ocean County since the day it was delivered. This Aherns-Fox model G-W-60-4, Reg. # 5035, has a 600-gpm and a small booster tank. The windshield was a later addition.

West Keansburg Fire Co. of Hazlet Twsp. received this 1955 Dodge Power Wagon WM-300 4x4 from the Freehold Independent, who had bought the truck from the Jackson Mills Fire Co. This truck first built for the NJ Forest Fire Service. A small truck with a lot of lives!

This Mack A hose wagon has proudly served Deal since 1950. The striping on this rig really stands out and it is a favorite in parades around Central Jersey.

76 Jersey Shore Fire Apparatus Volume 1 "Classics thru the 60's"

Cassville Fire Company of Jackson Township has this nicely restored 1946 Ward LaFrance 500-gpm pumper. This unusual closed-cab pumper presents an almost sinister looking appearance, with it's small windshield and cab design.

Built for just four short years (1950-1953), the Mack A was a hybrid of the L and E Models. This 505A rig was delivered to the Sea Grit Fire Department in 1953 and was painted in the traditional departmental color scheme of white. With it's red canvas top and fancy scrolled goldleafing, this is still a fine looking rig.

Jersey Shore Fire Apparatus Volume 1 "Classics thru the 60's" 77

It is very possible that this rig has undergone more changes than any other in New Jersey. Originally built in 1954 by American LaFrance on a 700 series chassis, this 1000-gpm quad also had 167-ft of ground ladder. It then had the water tank removed which made it a city service truck with a pump. By 1998 the water tank had returned and the life of this old star marches on.

Ship Bottom still owns this well preserved 1937 open-cab Ford/Pirsch 500-gpm pumper. This unit came equipped with a 200-gallon water tank. It's short wheelbase was well suited to this barrier beach towns small streets and driveways.

78 Jersey Shore Fire Apparatus Volume 1 "Classics thru the 60's"

Hope Fire Company of Allentown/ Upper Freehold Township, still owns this 1957 International R 190 chassis that was outfitted with a TASC body. This unit has a 750-gpm pump and a 1000-gallon booster tank.

This well kept 1954 International 17ASC pumper was in service until the 1990's, with the Ocean Gate Fire Dept. This unit had a 750-gpm pump and a 750-gallon water tank.

Not to be confused with the Ocean Township of Monmouth County, this 1956 Ward LaFrance 1000-gpm pumper is still in service with the Waretown Fire Company of Ocean Township of Ocean County. This unit came equipped with a 750-gallon tank.

The Howell Township Fire Company No. 1, also known as the Adelphia Fire Company, still has this 1942 Ford/ American LaFrance on the roster. It has been completely restored after many years of active duty. The unit is equipped with a 500-gpm pump and a 500-gallon booster tank.

Jersey Shore Fire Apparatus Volume 1 "Classics thru the 60's" 79

Some old fire trucks are able to stay around and get a second lease on life. This 1945 Mack 75 750-gpm pumper is based on the E series chassis. It came equipped with a 350-gallon tank, and was restored and maintained by the Rescue Fire Co. of the Lakewood Fire Department.

Wall Fire Co. No. 1 commonly known as West Belmar, still has this 1963 Mack C95 pumper. This unit was delivered with a ladder bank under the hose bed. The amount of ladders carried is more then a pumpers complement, however not enough to make this rig a true quad. I suppose you could consider this a "Baby Quad".

Complete with a white canopy convertible top this 1959 1000-gallon per minute Mack B pumper was delivered to the High Point Fire Company in Harvey Cedars, NJ, located on Long Beach Island. Carrying 1000-gallons of water this rig also also had a front suction for quick hook ups to hydrants. This unit is still in service.

One of the few open-cab apparatus still serving the Jersey Shore is Farmingdale Fire Company's 1961 open cab Mack C 750-gpm pumper. This unit has a 500-gallon tank, and was one of four open-cab Mack Cs rigs delivered to the shore, others included South Amboy, Highlands, and Toms River.

Dover Township's six companies make up the largest fire service in Ocean County. They have kept this 1949 Mack L 500-gpm pumper: in pristine condition. This pumper is equipped with a 500-gallon tank and is still operated by the members of Toms River Fire Company No. 2. It is a frequent participant at local musters and parades.

Jersey Shore Fire Apparatus Volume 1 "Classics thru the 60's" 81

The northern section of Dover Township is protected buy the Silverton Fire Co. The company still owns this attractive 1955 Ford / TASC 750-gpm pumper, with a 750-gallon tank.

Located in the northern section of Brick Twsp. is the Herbertsville Fire Company. In 1941 the Herbertsville Fire Co. took delivery of this Ford chassis with Hale bodywork. This unit came equipped with a 500-gpm pump and a 250-gallon tank. This style of Ford Chassis was used for one year only, before being redesigned for the 1942 model year.

This finely restored 1930 Mack Type 90 750-gpm pumper belongs to the Richardson Engine Co No. 2 of Freehold Borough. This unit is still brought to many musters and parades each year. This Engine Company was named in honor of Charles F. Richardson who is considered as the founder of the Freehold Fire Department in 1872.

Located just North of Seaside Heights is the barrier beach town of Lavalette. The town was named in honor of a U.S. Navy Admiral 1887. You can still find this neat little 1935 Ford / Pirsch resting on the apparatus floor. Pump capacity was 500-gpm while she held just around 300-gallons in her booster tank for fighting fires in the many seaside bungalows which makeup this community.

Hale Hale the gang was all called to Lakehurst, NJ in 1937 for the terrible Hindenburg Airship disaster. This 1934 Ford / Hale pumper is still owned by the Mantoloking Fire Company, which was one of many departments that were dispatched to the Navy airfield on that infamous day .

Jersey Shore Fire Apparatus Volume 1 "Classics thru the 60's"

Pleasant Plains Fire Company, located in Dover Twp. has kept this 1928 Reo Speedwagon. Built in 1928, this rig is today a favorite at local parades.

Manahawkin, NJ is a section of Stafford Township in Ocean County. Their Fire Company still has this 1924 Reo with a Hale pump and Hale body, it also has a 35-gallon booster tank.

Completely restored in the 1980's is this a 1926 Cosmopolitan pumper. Operated by the resort town of Seaside Heights, this rig saw plenty of action in it's day. Today her action consists of being taken out for parades and admired by passerby's and photographers.

84 Jersey Shore Fire Apparatus Volume 1 "Classics thru the 60's"

Surf City on Long Beach Island still has this 1957 Mack B pumper. This rig has a 750-gpm pump and a 500-gallon water tank. The Mack B was an extremely popular fire chassis after being introduced in 1953. During the last runs of this model Mack Trucks was so over run with deliveries that they secretly had Hahn build the bodies for them which were absent of any Hahn markings.

Still on the roster in Union Beach is this beautiful 1951 Mack 505 A 500-gpm pumper of the Union Hose Company. This unit has a 200-gallon water tank, and was put into reserve status in 1995. Note the post mounted beacon which was a common add on for Mack fire apparatus, due to the windshield design.

Jersey Shore Fire Apparatus Volume 1 "Classics thru the 60's" 85

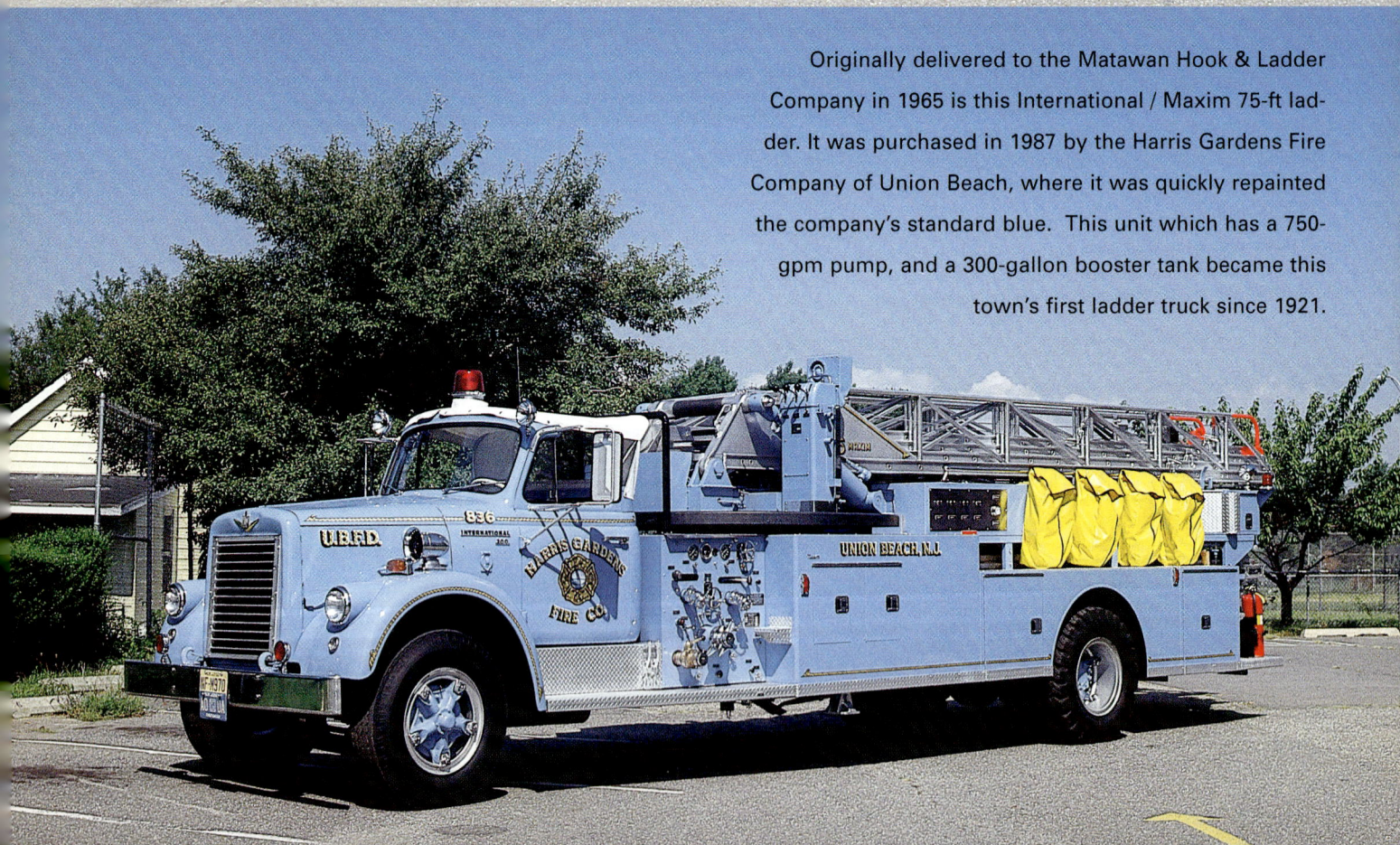

Ocean Grove badly needed to replace their aging 1928 American LaFrance tiller, so in 1964 the Eagle Hook & Ladder Company took delivery of this Pirsch 100-ft tiller. This unit is still in active service, albeit after a new diesel engine, and the addition of a closed-cab. It remains one of only two tillererd ladders left in service in Monmouth and Ocean Counties.

Originally delivered to the Matawan Hook & Ladder Company in 1965 is this International / Maxim 75-ft ladder. It was purchased in 1987 by the Harris Gardens Fire Company of Union Beach, where it was quickly repainted the company's standard blue. This unit which has a 750-gpm pump, and a 300-gallon booster tank became this town's first ladder truck since 1921.

Still serving with the United Fire Company in Neptune City is this 1954 Ford. Built by Great Eastern this rig is still considered a reserve unit.

This 1956 Seagrave 70th Anniversary Series pumper is assigned to the Union Fire Company of Belmar. This 750-gpm pumper which is equipped with a 300-gallon tank still holds a place in the apparatus room along with the company's steam engine.

Jersey Shore Fire Apparatus Volume 1 "Classics thru the 60's" 87

Great Eastern used a 1946 Ford chassis for the foundation of this small town pumper. Firefighting equipment consisted of a 500-gpm pump and a 300-gallon booster tank. This rig has been preserved and is still a proud member of the Tuckerton Fire Company in Ocean County.

88 Jersey Shore Fire Apparatus Volume 1 "Classics thru the 60's"

Bay Head Fire Co. still has this 1948 ALF 700 series pumper in service. This beautiful rig sports a 750-gpm pump and a 350-gallon tank. Other local rigs including Beach Haven and Manasquan's 700 series were sacrificed to keep life in Bayheads unit.

Delivered in 1947 to the Port Monmouth Fire Company, this Aherns-Fox model HT custom pumper is capable of delivering well over her rated 1000-gpm, the rig was extensively damaged in the 1960's. Rebuilt and restored, it still serves with P.M.F.C. in Middletown Township.

Jersey Shore Fire Apparatus Volume 1 "Classics thru the 60's"

Sea Girt just recently placed this 1956 American LaFrance ladder out of service. This rig had no pump and was equipped with a 75-ft ladder.

In 1958 the Ford Motor Company introduced their new Ford C Cab over chassis. This Cab was the same as the Mack N Cab which was designed by the Budd Company of Philadelphia. By the end of production of the Ford C in the Mid 1980's, thousands of fire apparatuses were built on these chassis. This 1965 Ford C/Hahn 1000 gpm pumper held a 500-gallon tank and was placed into service by the United Fire Company of Neptune City.

This nicely restored 1957 Ford/Great Eastern 500-gpm pumper is still owned by the Lanoka Harbor Fire Company. This attractive looking unit incorporates a 500-gallon tank.

LIBERTY HOSE CO. NO. 3

Delivered on September 24, 1952 this streamlined Ward LaFrance pumper was placed in service by the Liberty Hose Company of Keyport. Pumping capacity was rated at 750-gpm although everyone knew she could pump well over 1000-gpm when the big one hit. In 1978 a new Ward LaFrance replaced this rig, and the '52 was retired and placed on parade status only.

Keyport Fire Department's, Liberty Hose Company has just restored this 1929 American LaFrance pumper. This unit was replaced in 1952 by a Ward LaFrance, and was sold to the Doris Duke Estate in Somerset County. In 1996 Liberty Hose was able to buy back the old truck and add it to their antique collection.

This 1956 model EC Ahrens-Fox centrifugal pumper was equipped with a Waukesha 6 cylinder engine, a 750-gpm pump, and a 400-gallon tank. It still serves as a reserve until for the Oakhurst Independent Hose Co. of the Township of Ocean.

Eagleswood Fire Company, located in rural Southern Ocean County lies almost entirely in Bass River State Forest. Protecting part of that big area is this 1928 Hahn with a 500-gpm pump and a 250-gallon tank.

The rather small community of Ocean Gate, located on the Toms River, received one of the first Ward Lafrance pumpers delivered along the shore. This 1931 vintage apparatus came equipped with a 500-gpm pump, and a 300-gallon water tank. This rig is still owned by the town's fire company.

The Jackson Mills Fire Company of Jackson Twsp. still operates this 1955 Ford open Cab/Great Eastern (Oren) 750-gpm pumper, that was delivered with a 500-gallon tank.

Originally owned by Freehold's Engine & Hose Co. No. 1, this rig was later purchased by Marlboro NJ. Constructed in the American LaFrance Plant in Elmira, NY it was delivered to Freehold in 1928.

All three Hazlet Townships Fire Companies received new Ward LaFrance pumpers in 1956. Of the three only the North Center Ville Volunteer Fire Company rig survives. This unit was repainted Lime-Green after the delivery of the company's 1975 WLF Ambassador.

Contemporary Color

Another fine publication produced by the
Litho Tech Group

1.800.527.3765

BIBLIOGRAPHY

American Truck & Bus Spotters Guide 1920-1985 Tad Burness

The Complete Encyclopedia of Commercial Vehicles, G.N. Georgano

Seagrave Pictorial History, Matt Lee

Sanford Fire Apparatus, Joe Raymond, Jr.

The History of Fire Engines, John A. Calderone

American Fire Engines Since 1900, Walt McCall

Standard Catalog of U.S. Military Vehicles 1940-1965, Thomas Berndt

Mack A Living Legend of the Highway, John B. Montville

Fire Engines, Fred Crimson

Mack Fire Apparatus A Pictorial history, Harvey Eckart

Buffalo Fire Appliance Corp.,

an Illustrated History Peter D. West

International Trucks, Fred Crisman